DK WORKBOOKS

1st Grade

Math

Author Linda Ruggieri
Educational Consultant Alison Tribley

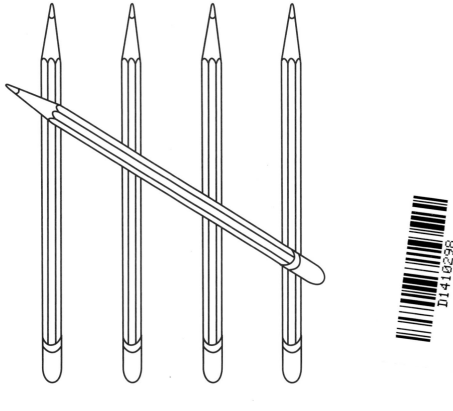

DK London
Editor Elizabeth Blakemore
Senior Editor Cécile Landau
US Editor Allison Singer
Senior Designer Marisa Renzullo
US Educational Consultant Alison Tribley
Managing Editor Christine Stroyan
Managing Art Editor Anna Hall
Senior Production Editor Andy Hilliard
Senior Production Controller Jude Crozier
Jacket Design Development Manager Sophia MTT
Publisher Andrew Macintyre
Associate Publishing Director Liz Wheeler
Art Director Karen Self
Publishing Director Jonathan Metcalf

DK Delhi
Project Editor Neha Ruth Samuel
Editor Nandini Gupta
Art Editors Dheeraj Arora, Rashika Kachroo, Baibhav Parida
Managing Editors Soma B. Chowdhury, Kingshuk Ghoshal
Managing Art Editor Govind Mittal
Senior DTP Designer Tarun Sharma
DTP Designers Anita Yadav, Rakesh Kumar, Harish Aggarwal
Senior Jacket Designer Suhita Dharamjit
Jackets Editorial Coordinator Priyanka Sharma

This American Edition, 2020
First American Edition, 2014
Published in the United States by DK Publishing
1450 Broadway, Suite 801, New York, NY 10018

A catalog record for this book is available from the
Library of Congress.
ISBN: 978-1-4654-1733-6

DK books are available at special discounts when purchased in bulk
for sales promotions, premiums, fund-raising, or educational use.
For details, contact: DK Publishing Special Markets,
1450 Broadway, Suite 801, New York, NY 10018
SpecialSales@dk.com

Printed and bound in Canada

All images © Dorling Kindersley Limited
For further information see: www.dkimages.com

For the curious

www.dk.com

Contents

This chart lists all the topics in the book.
Once you have completed each page,
color a star in the correct box below.

GOAL

Learn about groups of tens and ones.

1 ten   3 ones

How many ladybugs are there? **Remember**: First count how many groups of ten there are, then count the ones that are left.

 = [ ] tens and [ ] ones

 = [ ] tens and [ ] ones

= [ ] tens and [ ] ones

How many ants are there? Circle a group of ten, then count the ants that are left over. Write your answer in terms of tens and ones.

Tens	Ones

Learn to find groups of tens and ones.

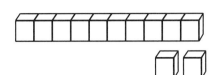

Tens	Ones	
1	2	= 12

For each problem, count the number of groups of ten blocks, and write that number under "tens." Then count how many blocks are left, and write that number under "ones." How many total blocks are there in each problem?

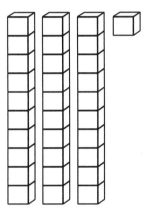 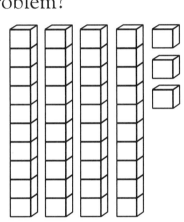 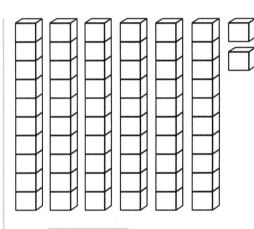

Tens	Ones
= ◯

Tens	Ones
= ◯

Tens	Ones
= ◯

Fill in the boxes and write the correct number.

	Tens		**Ones**	**Number**

2 tens and 8 ones = ◯ + ◯ = ◯

9 tens and 4 ones = ◯ + ◯ = ◯

3 tens and 6 ones = ◯ + ◯ = ◯

Write these numbers as tens and ones.

20 = ◯ tens and ◯ ones   72 = ◯ tens and ◯ ones

35 = ◯ tens and ◯ ones   17 = ◯ tens and ◯ ones

GOAL

Learn about adding
one more to a number.

$5 + 1 = \boxed{6}$

In each row, first count the smiley faces, then draw one more.
How many are there in each row now? Write the total number.

    +   = ⬚

 +   = ⬚

+   = ⬚

Complete the chart.

Starting Number	Add One More	New Number
9	1	
6	1	
4	1	
5	1	

Add the two groups of hearts. Write the total in the box.

♡ ♡ ♡ ♡ ♡ ♡ ♡ + ♡ = ⬚

Find out how to subtract one from a number.

 =    5 – 1 = 4

Count the number of objects in each row. Then cross out one.
How many are there now?

           7 – 1 = ◯

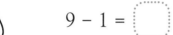   9 – 1 = ◯

Look at the pictures in each column. Circle the picture that shows one less.

   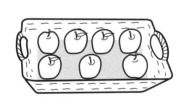   

Subtract one from the group of stars below.
Write the subtraction sentence.

      ✩ ✖

◯ – ◯ = ◯

GOAL

Learn to add ten to a number.

3 add ten = ⌜13⌝

Look at the puzzle pieces. Add ten to each number on the left. Then draw a line from each puzzle piece on the left to its matching number + ten on the right.

Remember: The number on the right must be ten more than the number on the left.

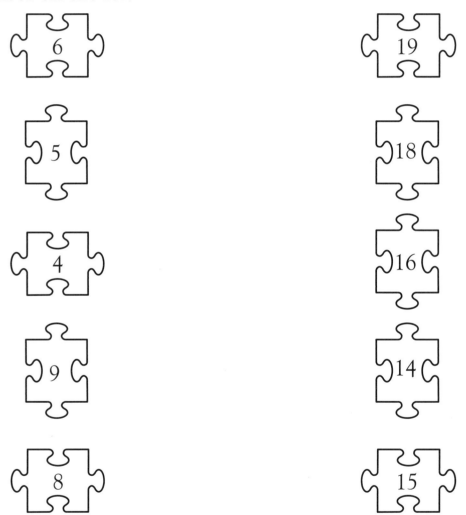

How many groups of ten are there in each number below? Write the answer in the box.

12　⌞　⌟　　　　35　⌞　⌟　　　　26　⌞　⌟

1234567891234567891

Learn to subtract ten from a number.   15 subtract ten = 5

Subtract ten from each number in the left column. Then write the subtraction sentence and the answer in the right column.

32 subtract ten   ⸤   ⸥ = ( )

28 subtract ten   ⸤   ⸥ = ( )

25 subtract ten   ⸤   ⸥ = ( )

56 subtract ten   ⸤   ⸥ = ( )

21 subtract ten   ⸤   ⸥ = ( )

36 subtract ten   ⸤   ⸥ = ( )

44 subtract ten   ⸤   ⸥ = ( )

18 subtract ten   ⸤   ⸥ = ( )

68 subtract ten   ⸤   ⸥ = ( )

95 subtract ten   ⸤   ⸥ = ( )

Finish the pattern. Write the number that is ten less each time.

50   40   ( )   10

GOAL

Learn how to add up to 10.

 = (10)

Read the addition sentences in each row. Then color the flowers using two colors to show the addition sentence.

6 + 4 = 10

8 + 2 = 10

7 + 3 = 10

2 + 8 = 10

3 + 7 = 10

4 + 6 = 10

9 + 1 = 10

5 + 5 = 10

Complete these addition sentences by writing the missing number.

4 + ( ) = 10   ( ) + 2 = 10   3 + 7 = ( )

10 1234567891234567891 2

Practice your addition skills.

 = 20

Help the clown reach the circus tent. First add each number sentence. Then follow the path of the number sentences with answers that are twenty or less.

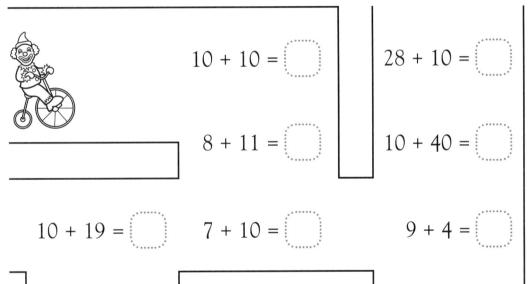

10 + 10 = ⬚   28 + 10 = ⬚

8 + 11 = ⬚   10 + 40 = ⬚

10 + 19 = ⬚   7 + 10 = ⬚   9 + 4 = ⬚

30 + 10 = ⬚

5 + 6 = ⬚

20 + 2 = ⬚

6 + 12 = ⬚

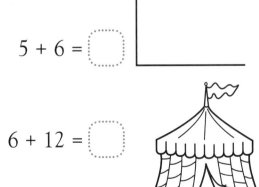

Draw groups of clown hats to show this number sentence: 3 + 3 = 6.

+   =

GOAL

Learn how to subtract with numbers between 0 and 10.

         5 − 3 = (2)

Look at the groups of fruit in each row. Then write the answer for each subtraction sentence.

         7 − 3 = ◯

      9 − 6 = ◯

        8 − 4 = ◯

         10 − 4 = ◯

        4 − 0 = ◯

Joan counted six oranges in her bowl. She ate two.
How many oranges were left?

Write the number sentence.

◯ − ◯ = ◯

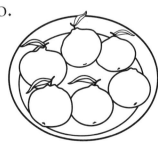

Practice your subtraction skills.

QQQQQQQQQQ⊗⊗⊗⊗⊗⊗

$$\begin{array}{r} 16 \\ -\ 6 \\ \hline 10 \end{array}$$

Subtract and write the answers in each row.

$\begin{array}{r}15\\-\ 4\\\hline\end{array}$	$\begin{array}{r}29\\-\ 6\\\hline\end{array}$	$\begin{array}{r}18\\-\ 5\\\hline\end{array}$	$\begin{array}{r}16\\-\ 4\\\hline\end{array}$	$\begin{array}{r}12\\-\ 2\\\hline\end{array}$	$\begin{array}{r}19\\-\ 3\\\hline\end{array}$
$\begin{array}{r}10\\-\ 7\\\hline\end{array}$	$\begin{array}{r}9\\-\ 5\\\hline\end{array}$	$\begin{array}{r}39\\-\ 4\\\hline\end{array}$	$\begin{array}{r}20\\-\ 10\\\hline\end{array}$	$\begin{array}{r}16\\-\ 8\\\hline\end{array}$	$\begin{array}{r}56\\-\ 6\\\hline\end{array}$
$\begin{array}{r}14\\-\ 7\\\hline\end{array}$	$\begin{array}{r}9\\-\ 6\\\hline\end{array}$	$\begin{array}{r}60\\-\ 30\\\hline\end{array}$	$\begin{array}{r}89\\-\ 9\\\hline\end{array}$	$\begin{array}{r}18\\-\ 15\\\hline\end{array}$	$\begin{array}{r}58\\-\ 8\\\hline\end{array}$

Read each story. Then write the answer for each subtraction problem.

Juan had thirteen crayons.
He broke two crayons. How many
of his crayons were not broken?

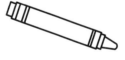

$13 - 2 = \boxed{}$

We saw twenty-five bunnies.
Four bunnies ran away.
How many bunnies were left?

$25 - 4 = \boxed{}$

Jen made nineteen cupcakes.
She gave away six cupcakes.
How many cupcakes were left?

$19 - 6 = \boxed{}$

1234 56789 1234 56789 12

GOAL

Learn to find the shapes that are alike.

Color in the shape that matches the first one in each row.

Circle

Square

Triangle

Oval

Rectangle

Color the rectangle red. Color the triangle blue.
Put an **S** on the square.

  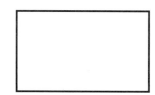

Learn to describe each shape.

A ☐ has four corners and four sides that are all the same length.
A △ has three sides and three corners.
A ○ is round.
An ⬭ has an egg shape.
A ▭ has four corners and four sides. Two sides are different in length than the other two sides.

Draw a line from each shape on the left to the object on the right with a similar shape.

In the box, draw three shapes in this order: square, triangle, circle.

GOAL

Learn how shapes are alike and how they are different.

A ◯ has no corners.　　　　A ☐ has four corners.

How many corners and sides does each shape have?
Remember: Some shapes have no corners or sides.
Some have three, four, or more corners and sides.

☐	△	◯
⬚ corners	⬚ corners	⬚ corners
⬚ sides	⬚ sides	⬚ sides
⬭	▭	⬠
⬚ corners	⬚ corners	⬚ corners
⬚ sides	⬚ sides	⬚ sides

Read the questions and fill in the missing numbers.

How are squares and rectangles alike? They both have ⬚ sides

and ⬚ corners.

How are circles and triangles different?

Triangles have ⬚ corners and ⬚ sides.

Circles have ⬚ corners and ⬚ sides.

How are circles and ovals alike? They both have ⬚ sides.

Learn how to sort shapes into groups.

This group has shapes with four sides.

Circle the shapes that belong in each group.

Shapes with no corners

Shapes with four corners

Write the answer to the mystery sentences.

Janette saw a shape with three sides. It looked like a slice of pizza. Which shape did she see? ....

Mike saw a shape with four sides. Two sides were short. The other two sides were longer. Which shape did he see? ....

Peter saw a shape with no sides. It looked like an egg. Which shape did he see? ....

Practice counting. This number line from 1 to 20 may help you.

1 2 3 4 5 6 7 8 9 10 11 12 13 14 15 16 17 18 19 20

Count the animals in each group. Write the number in the box.

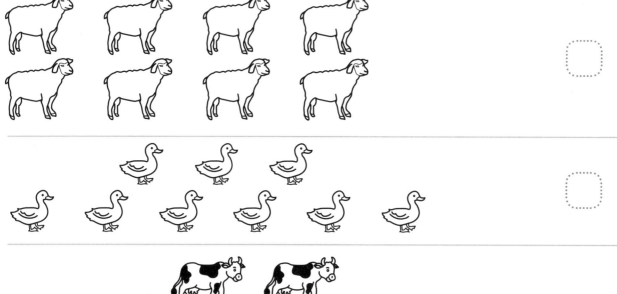

Can you count down? Write the missing numbers below the horses.

20 ⬚ 18 17 ⬚ 15

1234567891234567891 2

Learn to sort animals into groups.

This group has animals with stripes.

Circle the animals that belong to each group.

Animals with four legs

Animals with two legs

Animals with feathers

Sort the animals by writing the letter **F** under those that can fly.

....

GOAL

Learn that symmetry is when two sides of an object or shape look the same and are equal in size.

Draw a straight line to divide each shape into two matching parts. Then shade one half of each shape.

In each row, circle the shape that has a line of symmetry.

Draw a line of symmetry through each triangle.

 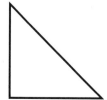

123456789123456789 12

Learn to fold shapes into
two matching parts.

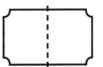

In each row, circle the shape that shows a fold line (----) that makes
two matching parts.

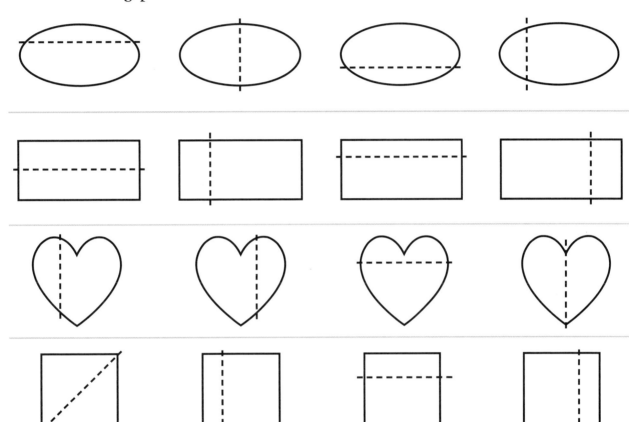

Draw a matching part for each shape.

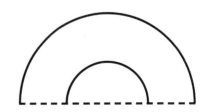

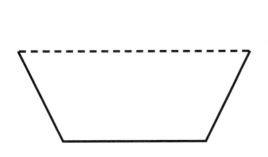

★ Recognizing Money

GOAL

Learn the names of coins.

1¢  Penny   5¢ Nickel   10¢  Dime   25¢ 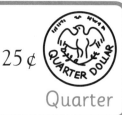 Quarter

Follow the directions in each section.

Circle four pennies.

Circle three nickels.

Circle five dimes.

Circle two quarters.

Circle two pennies and one nickel.

Circle three dimes and one quarter.

Read the amount of cents. Circle the coins that make each amount.

10¢ =

15¢ =

22 1234567891234567891...

Practice adding money.

$$25¢ \\ + \underline{12¢} \\ 37¢$$

Add the amounts of money in each row.

30¢ + 12¢	17¢ + 22¢	33¢ + 25¢	37¢ + 30¢	14¢ + 10¢
50¢ + 30¢	27¢ + 61¢	17¢ + 21¢	35¢ + 13¢	32¢ + 17¢
21¢ + 50¢	16¢ + 11¢	30¢ + 24¢	23¢ + 22¢	18¢ + 20¢
33¢ + 12¢	25¢ + 22¢	40¢ + 23¢	23¢ + 60¢	16¢ + 12¢

Look at each group of coins. Circle the one with the most money.

 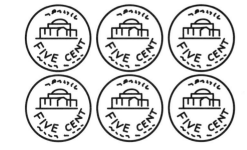

GOAL

Learn to double amounts.

$5¢ + 5¢ = \boxed{10¢}$

$$\begin{array}{r} 4¢ \\ + 4¢ \\ \hline 8¢ \end{array}$$

Look at the coins on the left, then draw the coins you need to double each amount. Add to find the total amount in each row.

   +  = ⬡

   +  = ⬡

    +  = ⬡

Write the answer to each addition problem.
Circle the equations that show doubled amounts.

$8¢ + 1¢ = \boxed{}$ $5¢ + 2¢ = \boxed{}$ $5¢ + 5¢ = \boxed{}$ $9¢ + 8¢ = \boxed{}$

$9¢ + 2¢ = \boxed{}$ $5¢ + 4¢ = \boxed{}$ $6¢ + 3¢ = \boxed{}$ $7¢ + 7¢ = \boxed{}$

Pam had four apples. Dan bought four peaches. How many pieces of fruit did they have in all?
Write the number sentence. $\boxed{} + \boxed{} = \boxed{}$

Is the answer a double?   ....

Find the coins
you need to use
when buying an item.

Look at the prices of the items. Circle the coins required to buy
the item in each row.

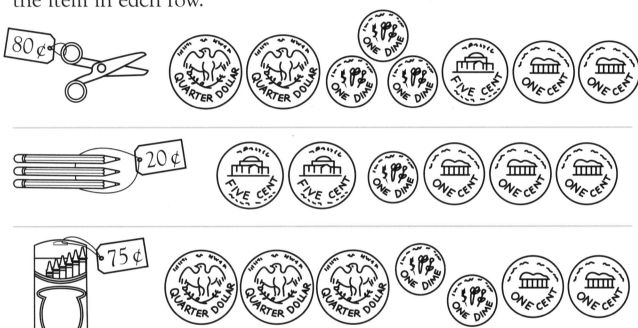

Draw a line to match the treat with the coins you need to buy it.

GOAL

Learn about getting back change.	You have	You buy 	Will you get change?
			(Yes) No

Count how much money you have, and write the amount in the box. Look at the price of what you buy. Figure out if you will get change, and circle "yes" or "no."

You have		You buy	Will you get change?
	☐	 25¢	Yes No
	☐	 35¢	Yes No
	☐	 15¢	Yes No
	☐	 55¢	Yes No

Jon has 35¢. He buys a toy truck for 24¢.

   How much change will John get back?   ☐

Learn how to calculate change using subtraction.

I have 20¢. I buy one apple.  I will get _5¢_ change.

Read each problem, and write the answer in the last column.

I have	I buy	I will get this much change.
50¢	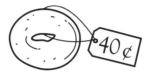	
70¢	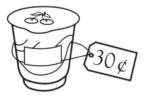	

Look at the prices of snacks given below. Then write the subtraction sentence and answer for each of the problems.

| yogurt 30¢ | bagel 40¢ | bag of pretzels 35¢ |

Sara has 50¢. She buys a container of yogurt from Mr. Jones. How much change should Mr. Jones give Sara?

Jill has 50¢. She buys a bagel from Mr. Jones. How much change should Mr. Jones give Jill?

Sei has 75¢. She buys a bag of pretzels from Mr. Jones. How much change should Mr. Jones give Sei?

GOAL

Learn to tell what time it is. This clock shows 2 o'clock.

The minute hand moves as the minutes go by.

The hour hand points to the hour of day.

Fill in the number to tell what time each clock shows.

o'clock   o'clock   o'clock

o'clock   o'clock   o'clock

o'clock   o'clock   o'clock

Fill in the correct numbers in the sentence below.

At 3 o'clock, the minute hand points to ⬜ and the hour hand points to ⬜ .

Learn to tell the time to the half hour. "Half past" means that it is 30 minutes past the hour. When you say "half past one," it is the same as saying "one thirty."

1:30

One thirty

Write the correct time for each clock in numbers and in words.

◯ : ◯

.... thirty

◯ : ◯

.... thirty

◯ : ◯

.... thirty

◯ : ◯

.... thirty

◯ : ◯

.... thirty

◯ : ◯

.... thirty

Write the missing numbers on the clock. Then complete the sentence.

It is half past ....

GOAL

Practice using the word *o'clock*.

.....3 o'clock.....

Look at each clock. Write the time each clock shows.

....

....

....

....

Draw the hands on the clock to show the correct time.

5 o'clock	1 o'clock	12 o'clock

1 2 3 4 5 6 7 8 9 1 2 3 4 5 6 7 8 9 1 2

Learn how to write
the time on a digital clock.

Write the time shown on the left onto the digital clock on the right.

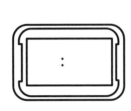

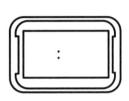

Write the time shown onto the digital clock face.

8 o'clock

six thirty

10 o'clock

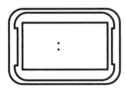
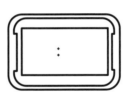
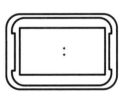

Show half past ten, or ten thirty, on both the clocks.

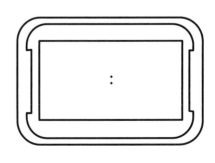

GOAL

Practice using clocks.

Jamie eats dinner at 5 o'clock.

Is it time for her to eat dinner?   Yes   No

Circle "yes" or "no" to answer the questions below.

John starts school at 9 o'clock. Does the clock show it is time for John to start school?

Yes   No

Look at the time on the clock. It is time for math. Does math start at 10:00?

Yes   No

Look at the clock. Reading starts in 1 hour. At what time will reading start?

Sam and his mom went to the store. They left for the store at 4 o'clock. They arrived back at home at 5 o'clock.

How long were Sam and his mother gone?   1 minute   1 hour

Look at the clock on the right. Lunch will start in half an hour. What time will lunch start?

1 2 3 4 5 6 7 8 9 1 2 3 4 5 6 7 8 9 1 2

Learn about how long it takes to do some activities.

The activity circled here takes more time than the other.

Circle the activity in each group below that takes more time.

Circle the activity in each group below that takes less time.

About how long does each activity take? Circle the best answer.

1 minute   1 hour   1 minute   1 hour   1 minute   1 hour

GOAL

Learn about the days in each week.
These are the names of the seven days of the week in order:

Sunday → Monday → Tuesday → Wednesday → Thursday → Friday → Saturday

Circle the correct answer for each question below.

Which is the first day of the week?   Sunday   Saturday

Which day comes before Wednesday?   Friday   Tuesday

Which day comes after Sunday?   Monday   Wednesday

Which day comes after Friday?   Tuesday   Saturday

July

Sunday	Monday	Tuesday	Wednesday	Thursday	Friday	Saturday
	1	2	3	4	5	6
7	8	9	10	11	12	13
14	15	16	17	18	19	20
☀21	22	23	24	25	26	27
28	29	30	31			

Use the calendar above to answer each question. Circle your answers.

What day of the week is numbered 1?   Thursday   Monday

What is the second Tuesday numbered?   9   16

Which date shows a ☀?   12   21

How many days are there in this month?   28   31

How many Sundays are there in this month?   4   5

Learn about the months of the year.

January	February	March	April
31 days	28 days	31 days	30 days

May	June	July	August
31 days	30 days	31 days	31 days

September	October	November	December
30 days	31 days	30 days	31 days

Use the information above to answer each question.

Which month comes after January? ....

Which is the month with the fewest days? ....

How many months begin with the letter J?

How many months have 30 days?

How many months have 31 days?

Which month comes between July and September? ....

Which month comes before June? ....

In the chart above, circle the month of your birthday.

Write the month of your birthday here. ....

How old are you? ⬚ years

Learn to find the length of
something using objects, inches,
and centimeters.

The crayon is three pennies long.

Each number marks an inch.

3 inches

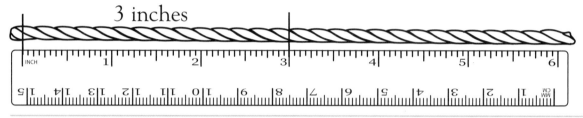

Each number marks a centimeter.

5 centimeters

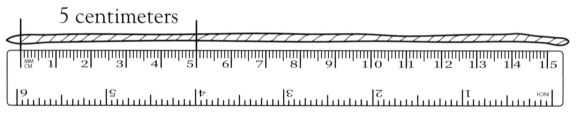

Measure using pennies.

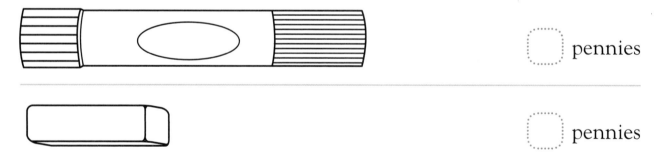

⬚ pennies

⬚ pennies

Use a ruler to measure this object in inches.

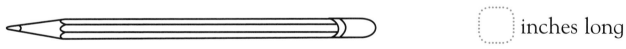

⬚ inches long

Use a ruler to measure this object in centimeters.

⬚ centimeters long

Learn to compare the lengths of things.

This bookcase is short.   This bookcase is long.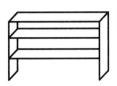

Circle the longer object.

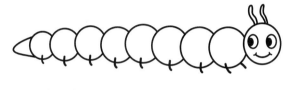

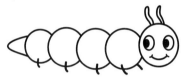

Circle the shorter object.

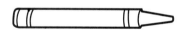

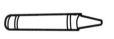

Color the shortest feather blue. Color the longest feather green.
Circle the other feather.

Learn about size.

The square with the circle around it is the same size as the first.

Circle the shape that is the same size as the first one.

Draw a teddy bear that is about the same size as this one.

1234 5678 91 234 5678 912

Learn to compare sizes, such as long and short.

The largest dog is circled.

Look at the animals and performers on the paths to the circus tent.

Path 1. Circle the largest.
Path 2. Circle the shortest.

Path 3. Circle the tallest.
Path 4. Circle the smallest.

Read each question, and circle the answer.

Which is heavier?

Which holds more?

GOAL

Practice making patterns.

Look at the pattern in each row. Draw the next shape(s) in the pattern.

Write the missing numbers in each pattern.

2   4   6   ☐   4   ☐   2   ☐   ☐

10   20   30   ☐   20   ☐   10   ☐   ☐

Make your own pattern. Use seven shapes or numbers.

A sequence shows the order in which something happens.

  1  2  3

Write 1, 2, 3, and 4 to put each story in the correct order.

 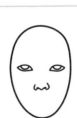 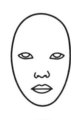 

Write the missing numbers in each squence.

20	19	18		16	

5	10		20		30

GOAL

Learn to read and use picture graphs to find the answers.

Frogs Tom and Matt Saw at the Pond

Tom	🐸 🐸 🐸
Matt	🐸 🐸 🐸 🐸

Matt saw the most frogs.

Use this picture graph to answer each question.

Dogs in Need of Homes

Black Dogs	🐕 🐕 🐕 🐕
White Dogs	🐕 🐕 🐕
Spotted Dogs	🐕 🐕 🐕
Gray Dogs	🐕 🐕 🐕 🐕 🐕

How many black dogs need homes? ☐

How many spotted dogs need homes? ☐

Which two kinds of dog are the same in number?

....

Of which kind of dog is there the most? ....

How many more gray dogs are there than spotted dogs? ☐

How many black and white dogs need homes? ☐

How many dogs are there in all? ☐

Write the subtraction problem and the answer. There are 15 dogs in all. People take 4 black dogs home. How many other dogs still need homes?

☐

1 2 3 4 5 6 7 8 9 1 2 3 4 5 6 7 8 9 1 2

Bar graphs show amounts or numbers of things by using bars of different lengths.

The bar graph shows the number of cakes a bakery sold in a day. Use the bar graph to answer the questions.

Cakes Sold in a Day

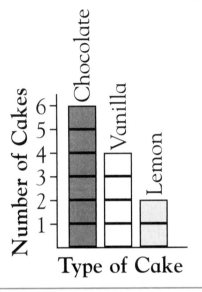

How many lemon cakes were sold?

Which cake did the bakery sell the most? ....

How many vanilla cakes were sold?

The bar graph shows the number of animals that live on Mr. Jones's farm. Use the bar graph to answer each question.

Animals on Mr. Jones's Farm

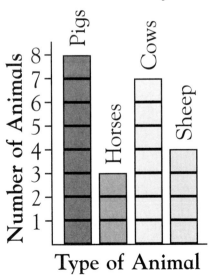

How many pigs live on the farm?

How many cows live on the farm?

Mr. Jones has sheep.

Mr. Jones has more sheep than ....

Mr. Jones has more .... than cows.

Use position words to say
where things can be found.

The fork is to the
left of the plate.

Follow the directions in each sentence.

Draw a cloud above
the rocket.

Draw a sun to the left
of the rocket.

Draw a planet to the
right of the rocket.

Draw a planet below
the rocket.

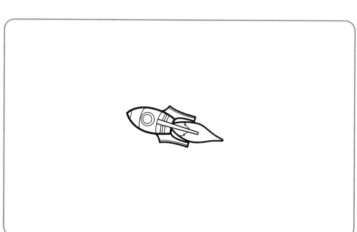

Circle the correct words to complete the sentences.

The bat is .... the ball.

near   far from

The fence is .... the house.

behind   in front of

The girl is walking ....

up the hill   down the hill

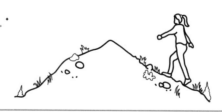

Read the clues, then write
each child's name under
the correct picture.
Kim is in the middle.
Tom is to the right of Kim.
Bill is to the left of Kim.

....

Use direction words to find your way. *Behind*, *right*, *left*, *in front of*, *between*, *up*, *down*, *above*, and *below* are some direction words.

Pam's dog has run off into the maze. Can you help her find him? Read the clues and draw a line to show her the way.

Clues

1. At the gate turn right.
2. At the ice cream stand turn left and pass between two apple trees.

3. Turn right and follow the path until you get to a bench.
4. Turn left, then right, and follow the path. Go up the steps.
5. Look behind the goldfish pond.

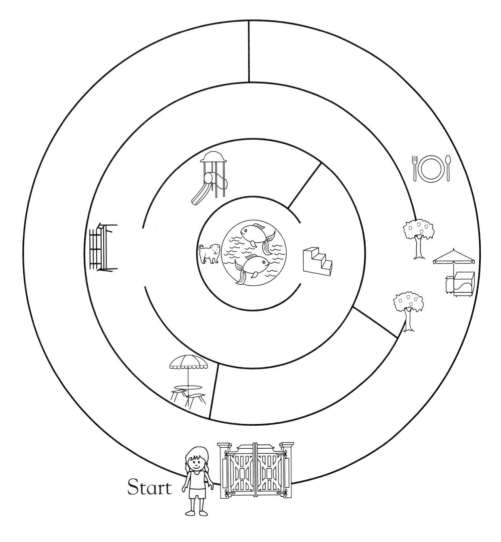

Start

Practice doing quick addition.

$$\begin{array}{r} 5 \\ + \ 5 \\ \hline 10 \end{array}$$

How quickly can you solve these equations? Ready, set, go!

| $\begin{array}{r}10\\+10\\\hline\end{array}$ | $\begin{array}{r}10\\+\ 5\\\hline\end{array}$ | $\begin{array}{r}10\\+\ 8\\\hline\end{array}$ | $\begin{array}{r}10\\+\ 7\\\hline\end{array}$ | $\begin{array}{r}10\\+\ 6\\\hline\end{array}$ | $\begin{array}{r}10\\+\ 3\\\hline\end{array}$ |

| $\begin{array}{r}8\\+\ 8\\\hline\end{array}$ | $\begin{array}{r}7\\+\ 7\\\hline\end{array}$ | $\begin{array}{r}9\\+\ 9\\\hline\end{array}$ | $\begin{array}{r}4\\+\ 4\\\hline\end{array}$ | $\begin{array}{r}5\\+\ 5\\\hline\end{array}$ | $\begin{array}{r}3\\+\ 3\\\hline\end{array}$ |

| $\begin{array}{r}6\\+\ 2\\\hline\end{array}$ | $\begin{array}{r}4\\+\ 8\\\hline\end{array}$ | $\begin{array}{r}2\\+\ 9\\\hline\end{array}$ | $\begin{array}{r}1\\+\ 4\\\hline\end{array}$ | $\begin{array}{r}8\\+\ 3\\\hline\end{array}$ | $\begin{array}{r}7\\+\ 3\\\hline\end{array}$ |

| $\begin{array}{r}9\\+\ 8\\\hline\end{array}$ | $\begin{array}{r}5\\+\ 9\\\hline\end{array}$ | $\begin{array}{r}8\\+\ 6\\\hline\end{array}$ | $\begin{array}{r}5\\+\ 7\\\hline\end{array}$ | $\begin{array}{r}18\\+\ 2\\\hline\end{array}$ | $\begin{array}{r}4\\+\ 9\\\hline\end{array}$ |

Add the three numbers in each equation.

| $\begin{array}{r}12\\9\\+\ 4\\\hline\end{array}$ | $\begin{array}{r}6\\5\\+\ 8\\\hline\end{array}$ | $\begin{array}{r}10\\5\\+\ 2\\\hline\end{array}$ | $\begin{array}{r}5\\7\\+\ 6\\\hline\end{array}$ |

GOAL

Practice doing quick subtraction.

$$\begin{array}{r} 10 \\ -\ 5 \\ \hline 5 \end{array}$$

Solve these equations quickly. You can do it!

$$\begin{array}{r} 6 \\ -\ 3 \\ \hline \end{array} \qquad \begin{array}{r} 7 \\ -\ 3 \\ \hline \end{array} \qquad \begin{array}{r} 29 \\ -\ 9 \\ \hline \end{array} \qquad \begin{array}{r} 9 \\ -\ 6 \\ \hline \end{array} \qquad \begin{array}{r} 16 \\ -\ 8 \\ \hline \end{array} \qquad \begin{array}{r} 7 \\ -\ 1 \\ \hline \end{array}$$

$$\begin{array}{r} 10 \\ -\ 2 \\ \hline \end{array} \qquad \begin{array}{r} 29 \\ -\ 7 \\ \hline \end{array} \qquad \begin{array}{r} 12 \\ -\ 6 \\ \hline \end{array} \qquad \begin{array}{r} 16 \\ -\ 4 \\ \hline \end{array} \qquad \begin{array}{r} 18 \\ -\ 10 \\ \hline \end{array} \qquad \begin{array}{r} 16 \\ -\ 6 \\ \hline \end{array}$$

$$\begin{array}{r} 18 \\ -\ 8 \\ \hline \end{array} \qquad \begin{array}{r} 9 \\ -\ 5 \\ \hline \end{array} \qquad \begin{array}{r} 16 \\ -\ 5 \\ \hline \end{array} \qquad \begin{array}{r} 17 \\ -\ 7 \\ \hline \end{array} \qquad \begin{array}{r} 16 \\ -\ 3 \\ \hline \end{array} \qquad \begin{array}{r} 19 \\ -\ 9 \\ \hline \end{array}$$

$$\begin{array}{r} 14 \\ -\ 6 \\ \hline \end{array} \qquad \begin{array}{r} 10 \\ -\ 6 \\ \hline \end{array} \qquad \begin{array}{r} 109 \\ -\ 9 \\ \hline \end{array} \qquad \begin{array}{r} 47 \\ -\ 7 \\ \hline \end{array} \qquad \begin{array}{r} 18 \\ -\ 9 \\ \hline \end{array} \qquad \begin{array}{r} 17 \\ -\ 10 \\ \hline \end{array}$$

Circle the number sentence that is related to $10 - 4 = 6$.

$6 - 4 = 2$ $\qquad\qquad$ $6 + 4 = 10$ $\qquad\qquad$ $10 + 4 = 14$

Certificate

1st Grade

Congratulations to

....

for successfully
finishing this book.

GOOD JOB!

You're a star.

Date

....

Answer Section
with Parents' Notes

This book is intended to assist children studying math at the first-grade level. The math covered will be similar to what children are taught before and during first-grade programs.

Contents
By working through this book, your child will practice:
- understanding the place value of tens and ones;
- recognizing the concepts of one more and one less;
- adding and subtracting objects and numbers up to 20;
- describing and comparing shapes;
- recognizing and adding money;
- telling and writing time to the half hour;
- understanding and measuring length;
- using picture and bar graphs;
- recognizing and using position and direction words.

How to Help Your Child
Your child's reading ability may not be up to the level of some of the more advanced math words, so be prepared to assist. Working with your child also has great benefits in helping you understand how he or she is thinking and where the stumbling blocks may be.

Often, similar problems and concepts will be worded in different ways such as, "count one more" and "which has more?" This is intentional and meant to make children aware that the same basic concepts can be expressed in different ways.

When appropriate, use props to help your child visualize the solutions—for example, have a collection of coins to use for the money problems, or find examples of objects to measure around your house.

Build children's confidence with words of praise. If they are getting answers wrong, then encourage them to try again another time.

Good luck, and remember to have fun!

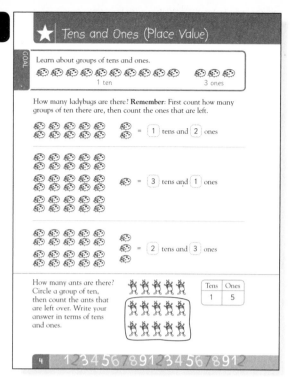

4 ★ Tens and Ones (Place Value)

GOAL: Learn about groups of tens and ones.

1 ten   3 ones

How many ladybugs are there? **Remember**: First count how many groups of ten there are, then count the ones that are left.

= 1 tens and 2 ones

= 3 tens and 1 ones

= 2 tens and 3 ones

How many ants are there? Circle a group of ten, then count the ants that are left over. Write your answer in terms of tens and ones.

Tens	Ones
1	5

Be sure children count groups of ten carefully. If they miscount a group of ten, they will reach an incorrect answer. You may want to have children practice counting tens and ones using groups of buttons.

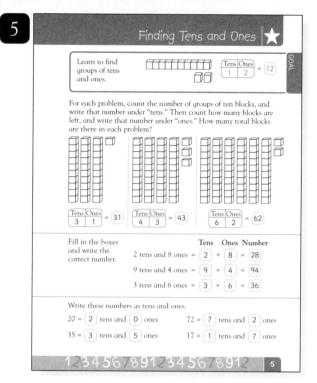

5 Finding Tens and Ones ★

GOAL: Learn to find groups of tens and ones.

Tens	Ones
1	2	= 12

For each problem, count the number of groups of ten blocks, and write that number under "tens." Then count how many blocks are left, and write that number under "ones." How many total blocks are there in each problem?

Tens	Ones		Tens	Ones		Tens	Ones
3	1	= 31	4	3	= 43	6	2	= 62

Fill in the boxes and write the correct number.

		Tens		Ones		Number
2 tens and 8 ones =		2	+	8	=	28
9 tens and 4 ones =		9	+	4	=	94
3 tens and 6 ones =		3	+	6	=	36

Write these numbers as tens and ones.

20 = 2 tens and 0 ones   72 = 7 tens and 2 ones

35 = 3 tens and 5 ones   17 = 1 tens and 7 ones

Be sure children understand that in two-digit numbers, the second digit stands for the number of units in the ones column, and the first digit stands for the number of units in the tens column.

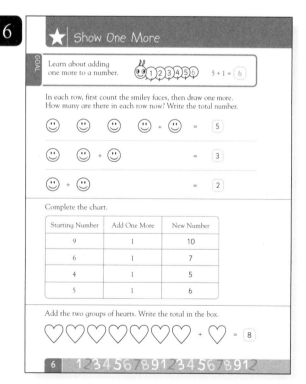

6 ★ Show One More

GOAL: Learn about adding one more to a number.

1 2 3 4 5 6   5 + 1 = 6

In each row, first count the smiley faces, then draw one more. How many are there in each row now? Write the total number.

☺ ☺ ☺ ☺ + ☺ = 5

☺ ☺ + ☺ = 3

☺ + ☺ = 2

Complete the chart.

Starting Number	Add One More	New Number
9	1	10
6	1	7
4	1	5
5	1	6

Add the two groups of hearts. Write the total in the box.

♡ ♡ ♡ ♡ ♡ ♡ ♡ + ♡ = 8

Use groups of clothespins to show a number. Ask children to count them aloud. Then add one more clothespin to the group of clothespins, and have children count aloud again. Clarify that the new total number of clothespins is larger because you added one more.

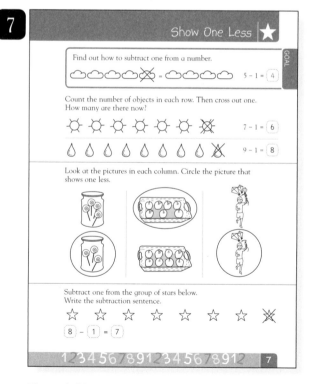

7 Show One Less ★

GOAL: Find out how to subtract one from a number.

5 − 1 = 4

Count the number of objects in each row. Then cross out one. How many are there now?

7 − 1 = 6

9 − 1 = 8

Look at the pictures in each column. Circle the picture that shows one less.

Subtract one from the group of stars below. Write the subtraction sentence.

☆ ☆ ☆ ☆ ☆ ☆ ☆ ✕

8 − 1 = 7

Show children a group of small toys. Let children count them. Then take one toy away, and ask them to count the toys again. Help them figure out and recite the subtraction sentence, such as, "five minus one equals four."

★ Find Ten More

Learn to add ten to a number. 3 add ten = [13]

Look at the puzzle pieces. Add ten to each number on the left.
Then draw a line from each puzzle piece on the left to its
matching number + ten on the right.
Remember: The number on the right must be ten more than
the number on the left.

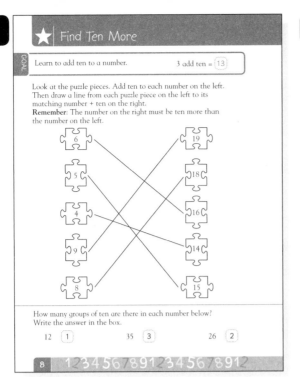

6   19
5   18
4   16
9   14
8   15

How many groups of ten are there in each number below?
Write the answer in the box.

12 [1]   35 [3]   26 [2]

Help children understand that ten more have
been added to the number in the first column
to come up with its match in the second column.
You can demonstrate the concept by using blocks.

Find Ten Less ★

Learn to subtract ten from a number. 15 subtract ten = [5]

Subtract ten from each number in the left column. Then write
the subtraction sentence and the answer in the right column.

32 subtract ten	32 − 10 = [22]
28 subtract ten	28 − 10 = [18]
25 subtract ten	25 − 10 = [15]
56 subtract ten	56 − 10 = [46]
21 subtract ten	21 − 10 = [11]
36 subtract ten	36 − 10 = [26]
44 subtract ten	44 − 10 = [34]
18 subtract ten	18 − 10 = [8]
68 subtract ten	68 − 10 = [58]
95 subtract ten	95 − 10 = [85]

Finish the pattern. Write the number that is ten less each time.

50   40   [30]   [20]   10   [0]

Use a set of dominoes to help children understand
subtraction: Have them count the dots on
a domino, then cover up one or more dots and
ask them to count again. Help children write
the corresponding subtraction sentence each time.

★ Adding Up to 10

Learn how to add up to 10.

🌿 + 🌿🌿🌿🌿🌿🌿🌿🌿🌿 = [10]

Read the addition sentences in each row. Then color the flowers
using two colors to show the addition sentence.

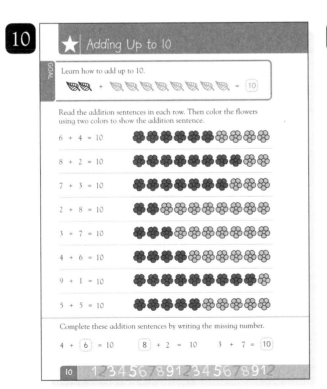

6 + 4 = 10
8 + 2 = 10
7 + 3 = 10
2 + 8 = 10
3 + 7 = 10
4 + 6 = 10
9 + 1 = 10
5 + 5 = 10

Complete these addition sentences by writing the missing number.

4 + [6] = 10   [8] + 2 = 10   3 + 7 = [10]

Have children first say the number sentence, then
count out the corresponding groups of flowers to
color. Create more number and coloring sentences
for children to complete using other objects, like
stars, suns, or balls.

Practice Adding Up ★

Practice your addition skills.

Help the clown reach the circus tent. First add each number
sentence. Then follow the path of the number sentences with
answers that are twenty or less.

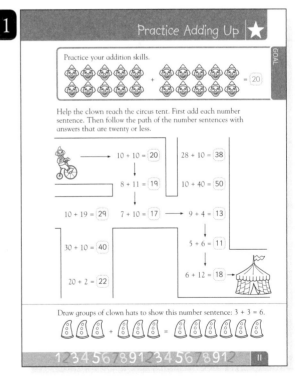

10 + 10 = [20]   28 + 10 = [38]
8 + 11 = [19]   10 + 40 = [50]
10 + 19 = [29]   7 + 10 = [17]   9 + 4 = [13]
30 + 10 = [40]   5 + 6 = [11]
20 + 2 = [22]   6 + 12 = [18]

Draw groups of clown hats to show this number sentence: 3 + 3 = 6.

You may want to ask children to rewrite each
number sentence on another piece of paper,
to practice and reinforce adding up to twenty.

12

★ Subtraction from 0 to 10

GOAL
Learn how to subtract with numbers between 0 and 10.

5 – 3 = 2

Look at the groups of fruit in each row. Then write the answer for each subtraction sentence.

7 – 3 = 4

9 – 6 = 3

8 – 4 = 4

10 – 4 = 6

4 – 0 = 4

Joan counted six oranges in her bowl. She ate two. How many oranges were left?

Write the number sentence.

6 – 2 = 4

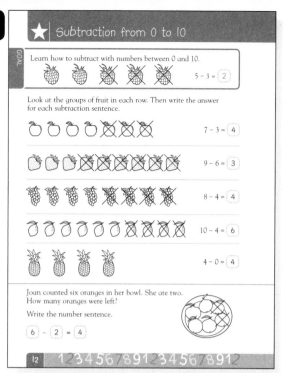

Place ten or fewer marbles in a jar. Have children count them. Then ask them to close their eyes as you remove a number of the marbles. Let them recount the marbles and write the corresponding subtraction sentence.

13

Practice Subtraction ★

Practice your subtraction skills.

16
– 6
10

Subtract and write the answers in each row.

15	29	18	16	12	19
– 4	– 6	– 5	– 4	– 2	– 3
11	23	13	12	10	16
10	9	39	20	16	56
– 7	– 5	– 4	– 10	– 8	– 6
3	4	35	10	8	50
14	9	60	89	18	58
– 7	– 6	– 30	– 9	– 15	– 8
7	3	30	80	3	50

Read each story. Then write the answer for each subtraction problem.

Juan had thirteen crayons. He broke two crayons. How many of his crayons were not broken?

13 – 2 = 11

We saw twenty-five bunnies. Four bunnies ran away. How many bunnies were left?

25 – 4 = 21

Jen made nineteen cupcakes. She gave away six cupcakes. How many cupcakes were left?

19 – 6 = 13

Write subtraction problems up to twenty on index cards. Write an answer for each problem on another index card. Place all cards on a table faceup. Let children match a problem card with the correct answer card.

14

★ Seeing Shapes

GOAL
Learn to find the shapes that are alike.

Color in the shape that matches the first one in each row.

Circle

Square

Triangle

Oval

Rectangle

Color the rectangle red. Color the triangle blue. Put an **S** on the square.

S

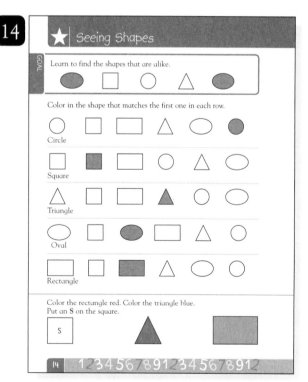

Go on a "Looking for Shapes" hunt around your home or neighborhood. Encourage children to find objects or lines that represent known shapes (circles, triangles, rectangles, ovals, and squares) and to call them by the correct shape name.

15

Describing Shapes ★

Learn to describe each shape.
A ☐ has four corners and four sides that are all the same length.
A △ has three sides and three corners.
A ◯ is round.
An ◯ has an egg shape.
A ☐ has four corners and four sides. Two sides are different in length than the other two sides.

Draw a line from each shape on the left to the object on the right with a similar shape.

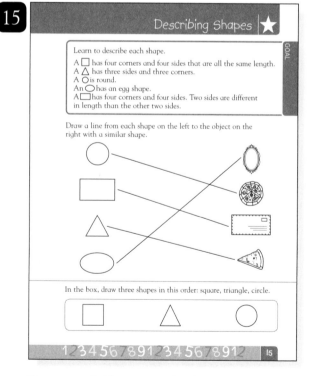

In the box, draw three shapes in this order: square, triangle, circle.

Encourage children to use the shapes they have worked with on this page to create pictures. Invite them to draw neighborhoods, playgrounds, shopping areas, and so on.

★ Comparing Shapes

GOAL Learn how shapes are alike and how they are different.
A ◯ has no corners.   A ▢ has four corners.

How many corners and sides does each shape have?
Remember: Some shapes have no corners or sides.
Some have three, four, or more corners and sides.

□	△	○
4 corners	3 corners	0 corners
4 sides	3 sides	0 sides
⬭	▭	⬠
0 corners	4 corners	5 corners
0 sides	4 sides	5 sides

Read the questions and fill in the missing numbers.
How are squares and rectangles alike? They both have [4] sides
and [4] corners.
How are circles and triangles different?
Triangles have [3] corners and [3] sides.
Circles have [0] corners and [0] sides.
How are circles and ovals alike? They both have [0] sides.

Let children create flat shapes from modeling clay. Ask them to make at least three of each shape on the page, each one a different size. Then have children order the three clay versions of each shape by size, either from largest to smallest or from smallest to largest.

Sorting Shapes ★

GOAL Learn how to sort shapes into groups.
▢ ▢ ▭ ▯   This group has shapes with four sides.

Circle the shapes that belong in each group.
Shapes with no corners

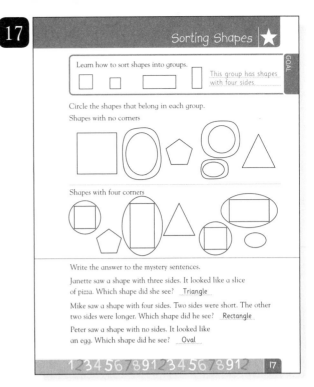

Shapes with four corners

Write the answer to the mystery sentences.
Janette saw a shape with three sides. It looked like a slice of pizza. Which shape did she see? Triangle
Mike saw a shape with four sides. Two sides were short. The other two sides were longer. Which shape did he see? Rectangle
Peter saw a shape with no sides. It looked like an egg. Which shape did he see? Oval

Help children find pictures of objects with the shape of a circle, rectangle, square, oval, and triangle in a magazine. Assist them with cutting out several pictures of each shape. Then let children sort the pictures into groups by shape and create a shape poster.

★ Counting Animals

GOAL Practice counting. This number line from 1 to 20 may help you.
1 2 3 4 5 6 7 8 9 10 11 12 13 14 15 16 17 18 19 20

Count the animals in each group. Write the number in the box.

[8]

[9]

[17]

Can you count down? Write the missing numbers below the horses.
20 [19] 18 17 [16] 15

Provide additional counting practice by placing a row of uncooked beans on a table. Remove several beans from their position in the row, leaving a space. Let children count aloud, saying the number of each missing bean.

Sorting Animals ★

GOAL Learn to sort animals into groups.
This group has animals with stripes.

Circle the animals that belong to each group.
Animals with four legs

Animals with two legs

Animals with feathers

Sort the animals by writing the letter **F** under those that can fly.
_____ F F _____ F

Provide children with small plastic animals. Invite them to sort the animals into groups by various characteristics (by color, with four legs, with two legs, with tails, and so on). For each group, have children explain the characteristic that they are using.

★ Symmetry

Learn that symmetry is when two sides of an object or shape look the same and are equal in size.

Draw a straight line to divide each shape into two matching parts. Then shade one half of each shape.

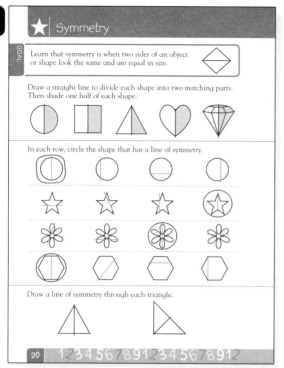

In each row, circle the shape that has a line of symmetry.

Draw a line of symmetry through each triangle.

Draw various shapes on index cards. Then cut the cards so that the shapes on them are divided in half equally. Mix up the cards. Invite children to find the matching halves and place them together.

Folding ★

Learn to fold shapes into two matching parts.

In each row, circle the shape that shows a fold line (----) that makes two matching parts.

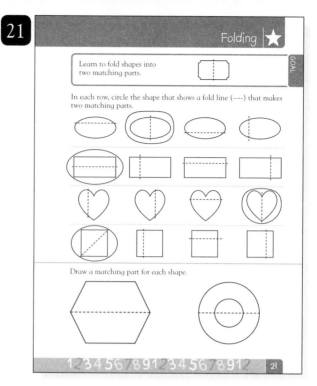

Draw a matching part for each shape.

Let children practice folding pieces of paper into equal halves. Explain that each side of the fold is a half. Have children color one of the halves, and help them understand that the fold is a dividing line, or a line of symmetry.

★ Recognizing Money

Learn the names of coins. 1¢ Penny 5¢ Nickel 10¢ Dime 25¢ Quarter

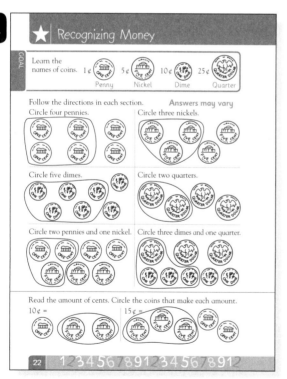

Follow the directions in each section. **Answers may vary**

Circle four pennies. | Circle three nickels.

Circle five dimes. | Circle two quarters.

Circle two pennies and one nickel. | Circle three dimes and one quarter.

Read the amount of cents. Circle the coins that make each amount.

10¢ = | 15¢ =

Engage children in coin riddles: Give clues to a coin you are thinking of, such as, "two of this coin makes two cents," (penny) or "two of this coin makes ten cents" (nickel). Let them work out what the mystery coin is.

Adding Money ★

Practice adding money.

$$\begin{array}{r} 25¢ \\ +\ 12¢ \\ \hline 37¢ \end{array}$$

Add the amounts of money in each row.

30¢ + 12¢ 42¢	17¢ + 22¢ 39¢	33¢ + 25¢ 58¢	37¢ + 30¢ 67¢	14¢ + 10¢ 24¢
50¢ + 30¢ 80¢	27¢ + 61¢ 88¢	17¢ + 21¢ 38¢	35¢ + 13¢ 48¢	32¢ + 17¢ 49¢
21¢ + 50¢ 71¢	16¢ + 11¢ 27¢	30¢ + 24¢ 54¢	23¢ + 22¢ 45¢	18¢ + 20¢ 38¢
33¢ + 12¢ 45¢	25¢ + 22¢ 47¢	40¢ + 23¢ 63¢	23¢ + 60¢ 83¢	16¢ + 12¢ 28¢

Look at each group of coins. Circle the one with the most money.

Write simple addition money problems for children to mirror using coins. For example, if you write "4¢ + 10¢," they could mirror the sentence by showing four pennies plus one dime, or four pennies plus two nickels. Let them count the coins to find the sum.

★ Double Trouble

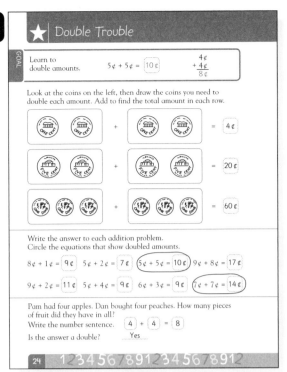

GOAL Learn to double amounts.

$5¢ + 5¢ = \boxed{10¢}$

$\begin{array}{r} 4¢ \\ + 4¢ \\ \hline 8¢ \end{array}$

Look at the coins on the left, then draw the coins you need to double each amount. Add to find the total amount in each row.

Write the answer to each addition problem.
Circle the equations that show doubled amounts.

$8¢ + 1¢ = \boxed{9¢}$ $5¢ + 2¢ = \boxed{7¢}$ $\boxed{5¢ + 5¢ = \boxed{10¢}}$ $9¢ + 8¢ = \boxed{17¢}$

$9¢ + 2¢ = \boxed{11¢}$ $5¢ + 4¢ = \boxed{9¢}$ $6¢ + 3¢ = \boxed{9¢}$ $\boxed{7¢ + 7¢ = \boxed{14¢}}$

Pam had four apples. Dan bought four peaches. How many pieces of fruit did they have in all?

Write the number sentence. $\boxed{4} + \boxed{4} = \boxed{8}$

Is the answer a double? ___Yes___

Let children practice adding doubles by creating doubles number sentences using buttons or paper clips. Help them add the doubles to reach the correct sum.

Shopping ★

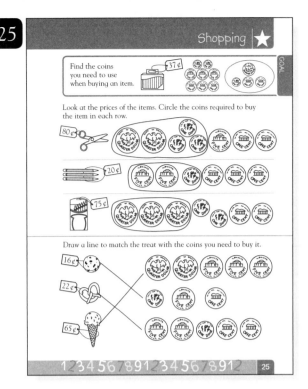

GOAL Find the coins you need to use when buying an item. 37¢

Look at the prices of the items. Circle the coins required to buy the item in each row.

80¢ (scissors)

20¢ (pencils)

75¢ (jar)

Draw a line to match the treat with the coins you need to buy it.

16¢ (cookie)

22¢ (heart)

65¢ (ice cream cone)

Place pennies, nickels, dimes, and quarters on a table. Hold up an object, such as a box of crayons or a small toy, and tell the children what it costs to buy. Let them find the correct coins from the money on the table to "buy" the object.

★ Figuring Out Change

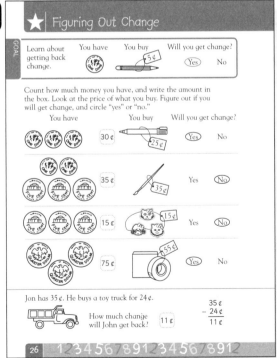

GOAL Learn about getting back change.

You have	You buy	Will you get change?
	5¢	(Yes) No

Count how much money you have, and write the amount in the box. Look at the price of what you buy. Figure out if you will get change, and circle "yes" or "no."

You have	You buy	Will you get change?
30¢	25¢	(Yes) No
35¢	35¢	Yes (No)
15¢	15¢	Yes (No)
75¢	55¢	(Yes) No

Jon has 35¢. He buys a toy truck for 24¢.

How much change will John get back? $\boxed{11¢}$

$\begin{array}{r} 35¢ \\ - 24¢ \\ \hline 11¢ \end{array}$

Remind children that they will receive change if the amount of money they have is greater than the cost of the item they are buying. Also have them practice writing amounts of money using the cents (¢) sign.

Giving Change ★

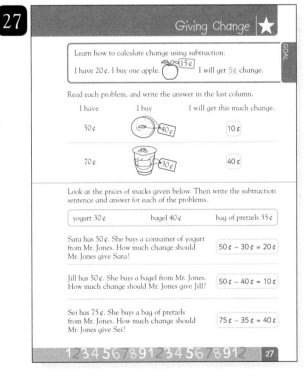

GOAL Learn how to calculate change using subtraction.

I have 20¢. I buy one apple. 15¢ I will get 5¢ change.

Read each problem, and write the answer in the last column.

I have	I buy	I will get this much change.
50¢	40¢	10¢
70¢	30¢	40¢

Look at the prices of snacks given below. Then write the subtraction sentence and answer for each of the problems.

yogurt 30¢	bagel 40¢	bag of pretzels 35¢

Sara has 50¢. She buys a container of yogurt from Mr. Jones. How much change should Mr. Jones give Sara? $\boxed{50¢ - 30¢ = 20¢}$

Jill has 50¢. She buys a bagel from Mr. Jones. How much change should Mr. Jones give Jill? $\boxed{50¢ - 40¢ = 10¢}$

Sei has 75¢. She buys a bag of pretzels from Mr. Jones. How much change should Mr. Jones give Sei? $\boxed{75¢ - 35¢ = 40¢}$

Ask children to pretend they have 99¢. Cut pictures of toys from magazines, and give each toy a price of less than 99¢. Children can select a toy to "buy," then subtract its price from 99¢ to find the change they would receive.

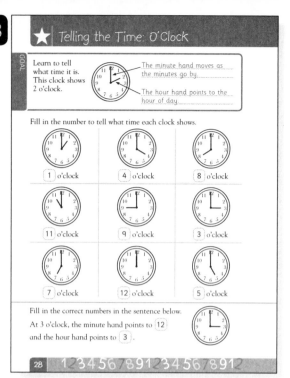

★ Telling the Time: O'Clock

Learn to tell what time it is. This clock shows 2 o'clock.

The minute hand moves as the minutes go by.
The hour hand points to the hour of day.

Fill in the number to tell what time each clock shows.

1 o'clock   4 o'clock   8 o'clock

11 o'clock   9 o'clock   3 o'clock

7 o'clock   12 o'clock   5 o'clock

Fill in the correct numbers in the sentence below.

At 3 o'clock, the minute hand points to 12 and the hour hand points to 3 .

Use a toy clock to help children tell the time. Say a time, and let them move the hands to the correct hour. Then have children say the hour and name an activity that might take place at that time.

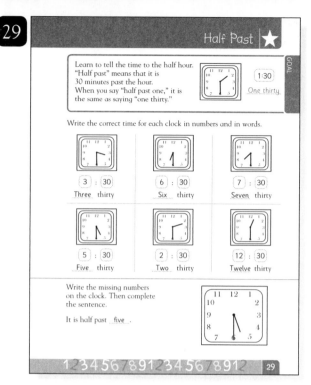

Half Past ★

Learn to tell the time to the half hour. "Half past" means that it is 30 minutes past the hour. When you say "half past one," it is the same as saying "one thirty."

1:30
One thirty

Write the correct time for each clock in numbers and in words.

3 : 30   6 : 30   7 : 30
Three thirty   Six thirty   Seven thirty

5 : 30   2 : 30   12 : 30
Five thirty   Two thirty   Twelve thirty

Write the missing numbers on the clock. Then complete the sentence.

It is half past five .

On index cards, write times to the hour and half hour. Place them facedown. Let children pick up cards and place them in the correct order from the time they wake up in the morning to the time they go to bed.

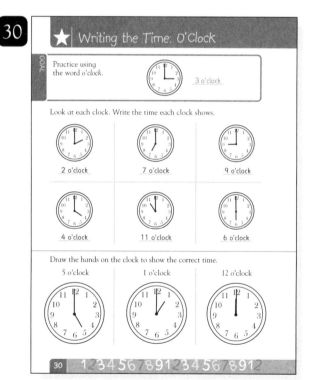

★ Writing the Time: O'Clock

Practice using the word o'clock.

3 o'clock

Look at each clock. Write the time each clock shows.

2 o'clock   7 o'clock   9 o'clock

4 o'clock   11 o'clock   6 o'clock

Draw the hands on the clock to show the correct time.

5 o'clock   1 o'clock   12 o'clock

On a toy clock, let children show times that are on the hour and on the half hour. Let them practice writing in numbers and words the time they are showing.

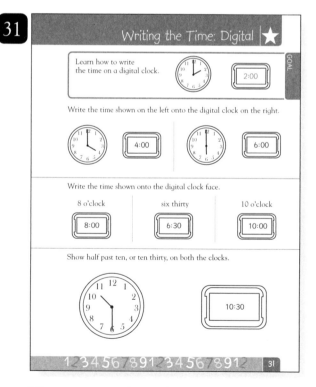

Writing the Time: Digital ★

Learn how to write the time on a digital clock.

2:00

Write the time shown on the left onto the digital clock on the right.

4:00   6:00

Write the time shown onto the digital clock face.

8 o'clock   six thirty   10 o'clock
8:00   6:30   10:00

Show half past ten, or ten thirty, on both the clocks.

10:30

Write times on index cards, using a colon between hours and minutes. Cut the cards in half, using puzzle-piece lines. Mix the cards, and have children find and put together the matching pieces. Ask them to write the time revealed on each matching pair in words.

★ Using Clocks

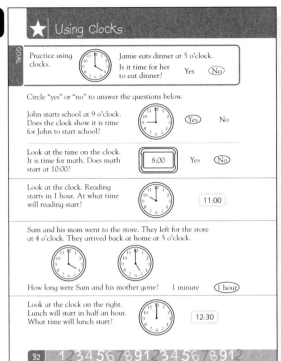

GOAL
Practice using clocks.

Jamie eats dinner at 5 o'clock. Is it time for her to eat dinner?   Yes   (No)

Circle "yes" or "no" to answer the questions below.

John starts school at 9 o'clock. Does the clock show it is time for John to start school?   (Yes)   No

Look at the time on the clock. It is time for math. Does math start at 10:00?   8:00   Yes   (No)

Look at the clock. Reading starts in 1 hour. At what time will reading start?   11:00

Sam and his mom went to the store. They left for the store at 4 o'clock. They arrived back at home at 5 o'clock.

How long were Sam and his mother gone?   1 minute   (1 hour)

Look at the clock on the right. Lunch will start in half an hour. What time will lunch start?   12:30

32   1 2 3 4 5 6 7 8 9 1 2 3 4 5 6 7 8 9 1 2

Draw analog and digital clock faces, showing times on the hour and on the half hour, on index cards. Mix the cards, and let children sort the cards to match the analog clock time with its corresponding digital time.

Differences in Time ★

GOAL
Learn about how long it takes to do some activities. *The activity circled here takes more time than the other.*

Circle the activity in each group below that takes more time.

Circle the activity in each group below that takes less time.

About how long does each activity take? Circle the best answer.

1 minute   (1 hour)   (1 minute)   1 hour   (1 minute)   1 hour

1 2 3 4 5 6 7 8 9 1 2 3 4 5 6 7 8 9 1 2   33

Discuss various other activities with children, and let them give an approximate time it might take to perform each one. As children practice assessing differences in time duration, they will become increasingly competent at judging lengths of time.

★ Days of the Week

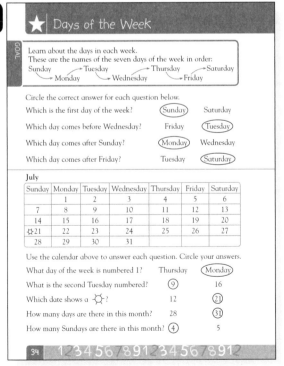

GOAL
Learn about the days in each week. These are the names of the seven days of the week in order:
Sunday → Tuesday → Thursday → Saturday
→ Monday → Wednesday → Friday

Circle the correct answer for each question below.

Which is the first day of the week?   (Sunday)   Saturday

Which day comes before Wednesday?   Friday   (Tuesday)

Which day comes after Sunday?   (Monday)   Wednesday

Which day comes after Friday?   Tuesday   (Saturday)

July

Sunday	Monday	Tuesday	Wednesday	Thursday	Friday	Saturday
	1	2	3	4	5	6
7	8	9	10	11	12	13
14	15	16	17	18	19	20
☼21	22	23	24	25	26	27
28	29	30	31			

Use the calendar above to answer each question. Circle your answers.

What day of the week is numbered 1?   Thursday   (Monday)

What is the second Tuesday numbered?   (9)   16

Which date shows a ☼?   12   (21)

How many days are there in this month?   28   (31)

How many Sundays are there in this month?   (4)   5

34   1 2 3 4 5 6 7 8 9 1 2 3 4 5 6 7 8 9 1 2

For additional practice, say the name of a day of the week, then ask children to name the day that comes either before it or after it. Let children check their answers by looking at a calendar.

Months and Years ★

GOAL
Learn about the months of the year.

January	February	March	April
31 days	28 days	31 days	30 days
May	June	July	August
31 days	30 days	31 days	31 days
September	October	November	December
30 days	31 days	30 days	31 days

Use the information above to answer each question.

Which month comes after January?   February

Which is the month with the fewest days?   February

How many months begin with the letter J?   3

How many months have 30 days?   4

How many months have 31 days?   7

Which month comes between July and September?   August

Which month comes before June?   May

In the chart above, circle the month of your birthday.
Write the month of your birthday here. ....
How old are you?   ⬜ years   **Answers may vary**

1 2 3 4 5 6 7 8 9 1 2 3 4 5 6 7 8 9 1 2   35

Have children repeat after you the names of the months of the year. Then talk about the weather where you live; let them choose different months and draw pictures to show what the weather is typically like during each of those months.

★ Length

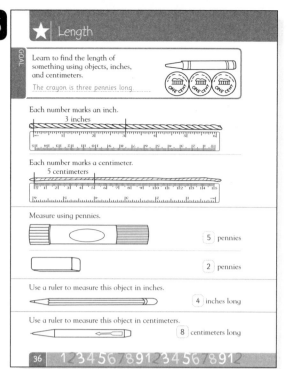

GOAL Learn to find the length of something using objects, inches, and centimeters.

The crayon is three pennies long.

Each number marks an inch.

3 inches

Each number marks a centimeter.

5 centimeters

Measure using pennies.

5 pennies

2 pennies

Use a ruler to measure this object in inches.

4 inches long

Use a ruler to measure this object in centimeters.

8 centimeters long

36 1 2 3 4 5 6 7 8 9 1 3 4 5 6 7 8 9 1 2

Let children practice measuring straight objects using a ruler. Help them understand where each inch and centimeter mark appears on the ruler. Have children write down the measurements, using the words "inches" or "centimeters."

Compare Lengths ★

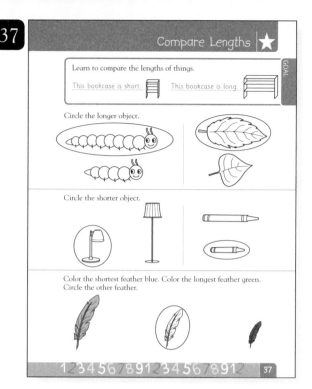

GOAL Learn to compare the lengths of things.

This bookcase is short. This bookcase is long.

Circle the longer object.

Circle the shorter object.

Color the shortest feather blue. Color the longest feather green. Circle the other feather.

1 2 3 4 5 6 7 8 9 1 3 4 5 6 7 8 9 1 2 37

Give children pieces of colored paper. Invite them to cut strips of different lengths that they can then label "long," "longer," and "longest." Children can then do the same activity, labeling the strips "short," "shorter," and "shortest."

★ Size

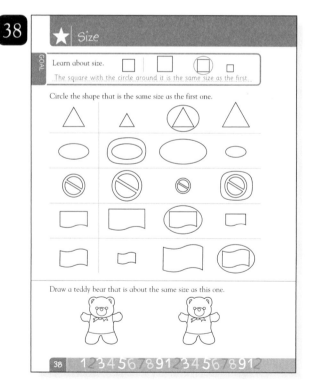

GOAL Learn about size.

The square with the circle around it is the same size as the first.

Circle the shape that is the same size as the first one.

Draw a teddy bear that is about the same size as this one.

38 1 2 3 4 5 6 7 8 9 1 3 4 5 6 7 8 9 1 2

Make sure that children carefully examine the shapes and their sizes. Explain that shapes can sometimes appear to be a different size because they are turned a different way.

Compare Sizes ★

GOAL Learn to compare sizes, such as long and short.

The largest dog is circled.

Look at the animals and performers on the paths to the circus tent.
Path 1. Circle the largest.
Path 2. Circle the shortest.
Path 3. Circle the tallest.
Path 4. Circle the smallest.

Path 1   Path 2

Path 3   Path 4

Read each question, and circle the answer.
Which is heavier?   Which holds more?

1 2 3 4 5 6 7 8 9 1 3 4 5 6 7 8 9 1 2 39

Show children hats, mittens, or boxes of different sizes. Let them indicate which is biggest or smallest, widest, thinnest, and so on. Do the same with other objects, letting children order them from smallest to largest.

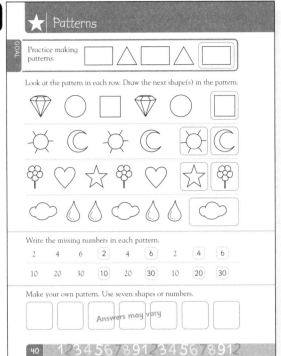

40 — Patterns

GOAL Practice making patterns.

Look at the pattern in each row. Draw the next shape(s) in the pattern.

Write the missing numbers in each pattern.

2 4 6 **2** 4 **6** 2 4 **6**

10 20 30 **10** 20 **30** 10 **20** **30**

Make your own pattern. Use seven shapes or numbers.

Answers may vary

Cut different shapes from a piece of paper. Arrange them in any pattern you wish. Let children add the next shape or shapes to extend the pattern. You can also draw objects in a pattern and let them complete the pattern by drawing the next object.

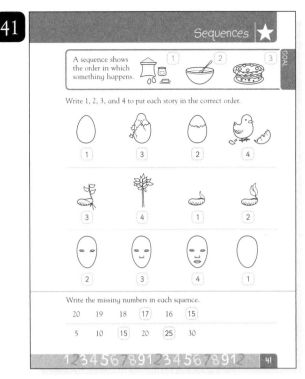

41 — Sequences

GOAL A sequence shows the order in which something happens.

Write 1, 2, 3, and 4 to put each story in the correct order.

1 **3** **2** **4**

3 **4** **1** **2**

2 **3** **4** **1**

Write the missing numbers in each sequence.

20 19 18 **17** 16 **15**

5 10 **15** 20 **25** 30

Explain to children that if someone is No. 3 in line, then he or she is in the 3rd position; No. 4 in line is in the 4th position; and so on. Then place a row of buttons in front of children, and have them say the names of each position from left to right.

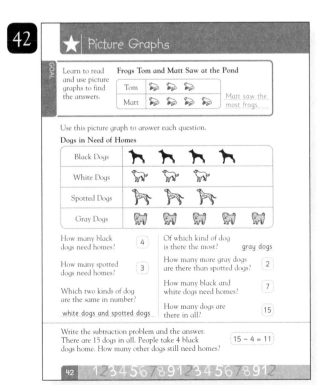

42 — Picture Graphs

GOAL Learn to read and use picture graphs to find the answers.

Frogs Tom and Matt Saw at the Pond

| Tom | 🐸 🐸 🐸 |
| Matt | 🐸 🐸 🐸 🐸 |

Matt saw the most frogs.

Use this picture graph to answer each question.

Dogs in Need of Homes

Black Dogs	🐕 🐕 🐕 🐕
White Dogs	🐕 🐕 🐕
Spotted Dogs	🐕 🐕 🐕
Gray Dogs	🐕 🐕 🐕 🐕 🐕

How many black dogs need homes? **4**

How many spotted dogs need homes? **3**

Which two kinds of dog are the same in number?
white dogs and spotted dogs

Of which kind of dog is there the most? **gray dogs**

How many more gray dogs are there than spotted dogs? **2**

How many black and white dogs need homes? **7**

How many dogs are there in all? **15**

Write the subtraction problem and the answer. There are 15 dogs in all. People take 4 black dogs home. How many other dogs still need homes? **15 − 4 = 11**

Help children understand that each picture on the picture graph stands for one object. Show them how to count each object in each row. When children understand this concept, ask questions like, "How many more black dogs than white dogs are there?"

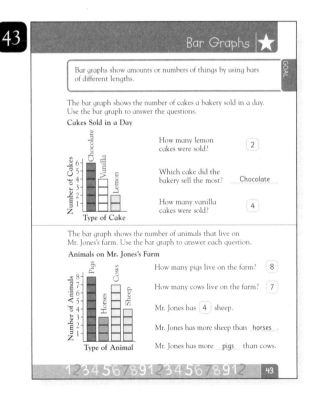

43 — Bar Graphs

GOAL Bar graphs show amounts or numbers of things by using bars of different lengths.

The bar graph shows the number of cakes a bakery sold in a day. Use the bar graph to answer the questions.

Cakes Sold in a Day

How many lemon cakes were sold? **2**

Which cake did the bakery sell the most? **Chocolate**

How many vanilla cakes were sold? **4**

The bar graph shows the number of animals that live on Mr. Jones's farm. Use the bar graph to answer each question.

Animals on Mr. Jones's Farm

How many pigs live on the farm? **8**

How many cows live on the farm? **7**

Mr. Jones has **4** sheep.

Mr. Jones has more sheep than **horses**.

Mr. Jones has more **pigs** than cows.

Explain to children that each box on the bar graph stands for one object. They can count the boxes in each bar to find the answers to the questions on this page.

★ Position Words

GOAL: Use position words to say where things can be found.

The fork is to the left of the plate.

Follow the directions in each sentence.

Draw a cloud above the rocket.

Draw a sun to the left of the rocket.

Draw a planet to the right of the rocket.

Draw a planet below the rocket.

Circle the correct words to complete the sentences.

The bat is _____ the ball. (near) far from

The fence is _____ the house. behind (in front of)

The girl is walking _____. (up the hill) down the hill

Read the clues, then write each child's name under the correct picture.
Kim is in the middle.
Tom is to the right of Kim.
Bill is to the left of Kim.

Bill   Kim   Tom

1 2 3 4 5 6 7 8 9 1 3 4 5 6 7 8 9 1 2

Write position words—such as "behind," "near," "next to," "to the left of," and so on—on index cards. Let children choose a card and use its word or phrase to describe where objects in the home are located in relation to other objects. For example, "The stove is *near* the sink," or "The mirror is *above* the dresser."

Following ★

GOAL: Use direction words to find your way. *Behind, right, left, in front of, between, up, down, above,* and *below* are some direction words.

Pam's dog has run off into the maze. Can you help her find him? Read the clues and draw a line to show her the way.

Clues
1. At the gate turn right.
2. At the ice cream stand turn left and pass between two apple trees.
3. Turn right and follow the path until you get to a bench.
4. Turn left, then right, and follow the path. Go up the steps.
5. Look behind the goldfish pond.

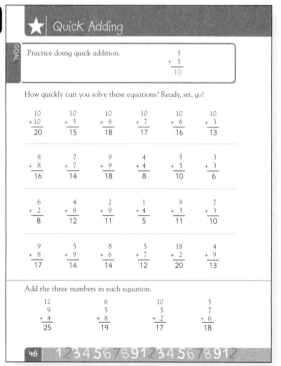

Start

1 2 3 4 5 6 7 8 9 1 3 4 5 6 7 8 9 1 2

Invite children to draw a house. When the drawing is complete, give them directions, using position words, on what to add to the picture. For example: "Draw a tree *next to* the house." Later, have children describe their pictures using position words.

★ Quick Adding

GOAL: Practice doing quick addition.
$$\begin{array}{r} 5 \\ + 5 \\ \hline 10 \end{array}$$

How quickly can you solve these equations? Ready, set, go!

10 +10 = 20	10 +5 = 15	10 +8 = 18	10 +7 = 17	10 +6 = 16	10 +3 = 13
8 +8 = 16	7 +7 = 14	9 +9 = 18	4 +4 = 8	5 +5 = 10	3 +3 = 6
6 +2 = 8	4 +8 = 12	2 +9 = 11	1 +4 = 5	8 +3 = 11	7 +3 = 10
9 +8 = 17	5 +9 = 14	8 +6 = 14	5 +7 = 12	18 +2 = 20	4 +9 = 13

Add the three numbers in each equation.

12 9 +4 = 25	6 5 +8 = 19	10 5 +2 = 17	5 7 +6 = 18

1 2 3 4 5 6 7 8 9 1 3 4 5 6 7 8 9 1 2

Try covering all the rows, except the one children are currently working on, with paper to help them avoid losing their place. Also help them learn quick addition facts through frequent practice, using flash cards or manipulative items such as marbles, paper clips, and blocks.

Quick Subtracting ★

GOAL: Practice doing quick subtraction.
$$\begin{array}{r} 10 \\ - 5 \\ \hline 5 \end{array}$$

Solve these equations quickly. You can do it!

6 −3 = 3	7 −3 = 4	29 −9 = 20	9 −6 = 3	16 −8 = 8	7 −1 = 6
10 −2 = 8	29 −7 = 22	12 −6 = 6	16 −4 = 12	18 −10 = 8	16 −6 = 10
18 −8 = 10	9 −5 = 4	16 −5 = 11	17 −7 = 10	16 −3 = 13	19 −9 = 10
14 −6 = 8	10 −6 = 4	109 −9 = 100	47 −7 = 40	18 −9 = 9	17 −10 = 7

Circle the number sentence that is related to 10 − 4 = 6.

6 − 4 = 2   (6 + 4 = 10)   10 + 4 = 14

1 2 3 4 5 6 7 8 9 1 3 4 5 6 7 8 9 1 2

Again, cover all the rows children are not currently working on, to help them keep their concentration. Frequent practice, using flash cards or manipulative items, is important for them to become quick at working out subtraction equations.